I0447435

Attitudes & Virtues

For a Directed, Balanced,

and Motivated Life

Tim Penner

Copyright © 2012 Tim Penner

All rights reserved.

ISBN-10: 1480017531
ISBN-13: 978-1480017535

DEDICATION

To my loving wife, Louise, for all her support.

To my wonderful daughter, Mary Lynn, for her graphic design work.

To George Waite, for his computer skills.

To Pamela J. Roark, for all her help and encouragement.

FOR YOUR INFORMATION

This pocket manual or workbook is loaded with insightful, common sense material. It will be a constant source of help, inspiration, and motivation.

"The greatest discovery of my generation is that a human being can alter his life by altering his attitudes of mind."
--William James, US Pragmatist philosopher & psychologist[1]

I always say, "Stay on course, do your mission."

---

[1] http://www.quotationspage.com/quote/1971.html

CONTENTS

CHAPTER 1
START NOW

You are a creation of God. Rejoice and be happy with your life because you have done some things well. With direction and encouragement, you will do even greater things. Oh yes, you have made mistakes. Who hasn't? Get over your mistakes. Move on in your **life's journey** and grow, overcome, share, encourage, and accomplish your mission.

As you attempt new and exciting adventures, the help you require will be there. **Have faith and believe**.

CHAPTER 2
YOU ARE HERE

You were born. You have one or more purposes for being here. Believe in your destiny.

More importantly, respond to your calling.

You are unique and that is clear. Do not look on others and compare. You may be poor and struggle to keep healthy, while the people with whom you compare yourself may be rich, healthy, and socially prominent.

The point is you are unique. God did not want a society of cookie-cutter people. Thus, to have a varied, happy and interesting world, there are people of different color, height, weight, language, etc. You must not form prejudices, but must live and work together. Love and appreciate others.

Keep on trying and doing. You are an inspiration to others. This is absolutely true whether you realize it or not.

CHAPTER 3
LIFE'S MISSION

We all have a mission or purpose in our life. Yours may be what you are doing now; or, it may be something you are contemplating.

It is your duty or responsibility to accomplish your mission. Missions can be simple (probably most are) or the mission can be of great magnitude.

Know your targets and goals. Stay focused on achieving them.

Example: Your mission can be your family, job, church position, or special project.

It is exciting, rewarding, and extremely fulfilling when you are "on track" and accomplishing your mission.

Be results oriented.

CHAPTER 4
TRUTH

Please believe that everyone on this planet earth encounters problems. Problems like: addiction, bad bosses, complaints, debt, embarrassment, fear, grouches, handicap, inferiority complex, job issues, and much more.

No one is exempt from problems. They are a natural occurrence in our **life's journey**. You must **overcome** your particular or unique problems.

CHAPTER 5
OVERCOMING

Overcoming a problem whether it be an addiction, financial set-back, surgery, job issue, or whatever is crucial to your well-being and success. Overcoming a particular problem is accomplished by maintaining your "can do" attitude and putting a routine or program together. If necessary, consult and confide with a coach or a close friend and most importantly – pray for strength and guidance.

"If God is for us, who can be against us?"
Romans 8:31[2]

Respond to the challenge.

---

[2] THE HOLY BIBLE, NEW INTERNATIONAL VERSION®, NIV® Copyright © 1973, 1978, 1984, 2011 by Biblica, Inc.™ Used by permission. All rights reserved worldwide.

CHAPTER 6
DIRECTED AND BALANCED LIFE

A directed and balanced life is one in which a person actually lives, uses, shares, and performs in all areas or sectors of his/her life. Doing this is simply staying in harmony with nature's plan.

Main areas of one's life are:

- Spiritual
- Personal
- Family
- Physical
- Work
- School
- Church
- Social

CHAPTER 7
ATTITUDE

Attitude is how we feel, believe, and react to the events, conditions, and situations in all areas of our life. i.e. home, work, school, church, social, etc.

It is important to know that the choice to have a positive attitude is yours.

Keep yourself thinking "positive" thoughts, despite how easy it is to think fearful or "I cannot do this" thoughts.

Have a period of meditative and reflective thought to get yourself in a proper frame of mind.

Be enthusiastic about your life, family, work, church.

Keep your eye on the target or goal.

CHAPTER 8
MAIN ELEMENTS THAT FORM OUR ATTITUDE

1. Personality and emotional make-up
2. How we listen and communicate
3. Belief level
4. Self-discipline
5. "Gratitude" level
6. Values
7. Goals

It takes EFFORT to form a healthy ATTITUDE. Work on it.

CHAPTER 9
HOW TO KEEP YOUR
ATTITUDE POSITIVE

1. Have a deep **faith**.
2. **Trust** in your ability.
3. Remember to **act**.
4. **Never give up**.
5. **Pray**. Do contemplative prayer, and **meditate**.
6. There is always **help** when you need it.
7. Be **enthusiastic** about your challenges.
8. Be **rested** and **healthy**.
9. **Listen** to others and **communicate** with **respect** and **understanding**.
10. Remember: **overcoming** is part of your journey.
11. Utilize **time management** principles.
12. **Dedication** and **discipline**.

CHAPTER 10
INPUT/OUTPUT

Just as the computer industry says "garbage in, garbage out," so too goes the operation of our **thinking** and **actions**. It is logical and easy to understand: What goes in, comes out. You cannot put lead into a mold and get a gold coin.

Again, what you put into your human machine (brain and body) cannot help but manifest itself into your speech, actions, looks, and health.

As James Allen stated in his wonderful work, *As A Man Thinketh*, "Good thoughts and actions can never produce bad results; bad thoughts and actions can never produce good results."
James Allen[3]

---

[3] Allen, James. *As A Man Thinketh*. Philadelphia: Running Press, 1989. Print.

CHAPTER 11
CONDUCT OF LIFE

In all matters, conduct your life with the highest of ideals and integrity.

Focus and work on your immediate tasks and main mission.

Reach high, but remain realistic in your expectations. Also, some things just take time, so have tenacity and patience.

Try to **act** as compared to **react**.

CHAPTER 12
SPIRITUAL STRENGTH

The world needs and is crying out for people who are spiritually and mentally tough. For people who have the courage to do the right thing, and stand by their convictions under the never ending negative influences of our society. Doing this is true leadership. **We can all be leaders in the cause for right and truth**. We grow as individuals when we act and conduct ourselves according to basic human ethics.

CHAPTER 13
SOCIETY'S NEGATIVE INFLUENCES

There is nothing wrong with movies, radio, and television. They are our main sources of non-personal input and entertainment. However, you must be careful not to be easily influenced by the sometimes lack of values and morals that are so common in these forms of input and entertainment. Maintain your high standards not only for yourself, but for the example you set for others. **Whether you realize it or not, others notice your actions. You are a model for others. Be a good model.**

CHAPTER 14
THE ENEMY WITHIN

Sometimes we are so busy or hung up on watching ourselves from outside influences that we forget that the enemy may be within the gates.

In other words, keep your yourself free from petty faults like jealousy, unrealistic fantasies, negative thinking and laziness.

CHAPTER 15
DID YOU REALLY MESS-UP?

Do not fret if you really blew it in terms of family situation, job, career move, or business opportunity. If the situation calls for it, apologize. Then forget it. If called for, provide restitution. Ask God for forgiveness. **God will forgive you. Now, forgive yourself.** If God could forgive you, you certainly must forgive yourself. Do not go through life beating yourself up. Beating yourself up takes away valuable time and energy and accomplishes nothing. **You have more to do than waste precious time, energy, and talent.**

CHAPTER 16
PROBLEM SOLVING

Here is how you solve a problem:

1. Analyze what is truly the problem.
2. Determine the cause of the problem.
3. List possible solutions to solve the problem.
4. Review and select the best solution.
5. Implement the solution.
6. Monitor the situation to ensure the problem does not repeat.
7. If needed, get professional help.

CHAPTER 17
VALUES FOR A DIRECTED AND BALANCED LIFE

1   Morals, Values, and Spiritual Principles
2   Knowledge of your mission
3   Goals and Targets
4   Perseverance
5   Discipline
6   Positive Attitude
7   Gratitude
8   Enjoy Life
9   Do the Right Thing
10 Faith (Belief), Hope, and Love

CHAPTER 18
MORALS, VALUES, AND
SPIRITUAL PRINCIPLES

Let your **morals** reflect Judeo-Christian Concepts. **The Ten Commandments, The Beatitudes, and The Golden Rule.** Value life. Life is priceless. Life is meant to be meaningful. **Make a difference.**

Spiritual principles – Live your life spiritually as well as physically. There is a "chart" kept on everyone. Believe this and live accordingly. Pray and do contemplative prayer daily.

CHAPTER 19
KNOW AND DO YOUR MISSION

Everyone has a job to do. More specifically, everyone has a specific mission. What is yours?

Keep in mind that all missions are not earth-shattering. Most are not. **That's O.K.**

Act upon yours, as it is the main reason you are here. **Performing your mission is the path to true inner happiness**. As mentioned before, your mission can be your family, job, church position, special project, or whatever is most important to you.

If you do not know your mission, search your soul for insight. Pray for direction.

Remember my mantra: **stay on course, do your mission.**

CHAPTER 20
GOALS

If you are not aiming at the target, chances are you will not hit the target.

Setting goals is an act of personal affirmation and conviction. Goals show you believe in yourself as well as your pursuits.

A time schedule for accomplishing your goal is important, as it keeps you motivated and helps prevent procrastination.

Goals stimulate thinking and generate action.

CHAPTER 21
PERSEVERANCE

People who succeed or overcome do not let the conditions of events, opinions, hear-say, poor grades, or lack of money alter their basic attitudinal belief in themselves and what they want to accomplish in their lives.

Successful people believe in themselves and their purpose/mission in life. They realize they have something to offer the world, their family, workplace, church, or club.

As William Arthur Ward stated[4], there are Four Steps to Achievement:
1. Plan Purposely.
2. Prepare Prayerfully.
3. Proceed Positively.
4. Pursue Persistently.

Know what you want. Find out what it takes to get it. Act on it and **persevere**.

---

[4] Dictionary of Quotes. 2008-2012. http://www.dictionary-quotes.com/four-steps-to-achievement-plan-purposefully-prepare-prayerfully-proceed-positively-pursue-persistently-william-arthur-ward/

CHAPTER 22
A VIEWPOINT ON PERSEVERANCE

"It is not the critic who counts; not the man who points out how the strong man stumbles or where the doer of deeds could have done better. The credit belongs to the man who is actually in the arena, whose face is marred by dust and sweat and blood, who strives valiantly; who errs and comes up short again and again; because there is no effort without error or shortcoming; but who knows the great enthusiasms, the great devotions, who spends himself for a worthy cause; who, at the best, knows, in the end, the triumph of high achievement, and who, at the worst, if he fails, at least he fails while daring greatly, so that his place shall never be with those cold and timid souls who knew neither victory nor defeat."

Theodore Roosevelt[5], 26th U.S. President

[5] Moncur, Michael. The Quotations Page.
http://www.quotationspage.com/quote/4758.html Web. 7 April 2012.

CHAPTER 23
PERSISTENCE

"Nothing in the world can take the place of persistence. Talent will not; nothing is more common than unsuccessful men with talent. Genius will not; unrewarded genius is almost a proverb. Education will not; the world is full of educated derelicts. **Persistence** and **determination** alone are omnipotent. The slogan 'Press On' has solved and always will solve the problems of the human race."

Calvin Coolidge[6], 30th U.S. President

[6] Moncur, Michael. The Quotations Page.
http://www.quotationspage.com/quote/2771.html Web. 7 April 2012.

CHAPTER 24
DISCIPLINE

Keep to the laws of society as well as your own self-imposed guidelines. Do this all the time. **Have integrity**.

Develop good habits like:

1. Eat healthily.
2. Do tough jobs first.
3. Have a good work ethic.
4. Practice being cheerful.
5. Read uplifting material.
6. If someone needs help, help them.
7. Maintain positive thoughts.
8. Save some of your money.

Discipline means you are your own boss.
You depend on yourself.
Do what must be done and you persevere.

CHAPTER 25
DO THE RIGHT THING

Let's face it. You know what is right and what is wrong...
do the right thing.

It is not the law to help your widow neighbor rake her
leaves, but it is the nice thing to do—the right thing to do. It
is not the law to help a charity, but it is the right thing to do.

Help others, share with others, **encourage others**.

When you encourage someone, you are instilling courage in
them. **People need encouragement.**

CHAPTER 26
GRATITUDE

Be thankful for what you have. For a moment, just suppose you did not have your family, friends, job, hobby, and your present level of health. Things would sure be different, do you agree?

What if your current job is not your ideal or dream job? First, be thankful for it. Second, you may be able to turn that position into something great, fruitful, and exciting. Third, you can change jobs if you feel that is the answer. Or, four, you can start your own company.

All of the above takes true desire, effort, and planning.

If you need a friend, be a friend first. Join a church group, hobby association, or do volunteer work at a hospital, recreation center, church, or school.

Remember to be supportive and encouraging to people. We should be like a lit candle in the world, continuously lighting others with love and understanding.

This action will make the world a better place and the love and understanding will be returned. Like the law of physics, for every action, there is an equal and opposite reaction.

Paraphrasing a verse in the Bible: **As you sow, so shall you reap.** 2 Corinthians 9:6[7]

Gratitude brings out the reality of what you have. It reminds one to say: Thank you God.

[7] THE HOLY BIBLE, NEW INTERNATIONAL VERSION®, NIV® Copyright © 1973, 1978, 1984, 2011 by Biblica, Inc.™ Used by permission. All rights reserved worldwide.

CHAPTER 27
ENJOY LIFE

"There is a time for everything, and a season for every activity under the heavens: a time to be born and a time to die, a time to plant and a time to uproot... "
Ecclesiastes 3:1-3[8]

Stay interested in life and all its wonders. These wonders are to be appreciated.

Never stop growing, learning, searching, and building. These activities will keep you alert, motivated, and directed. You will find life worthwhile and fascinating.

Get a cup of coffee with a friend. Start a book review group. Start a new hobby. Challenge yourself.

Relax. Give yourself a time to re-charge your energy cells. Doing this makes you fresh, and ready to meet the challenges of your life.

---

[8] THE HOLY BIBLE, NEW INTERNATIONAL VERSION®, NIV® Copyright © 1973, 1978, 1984, 2011 by Biblica, Inc.™ Used by permission. All rights reserved worldwide.

CHAPTER 28
FAITH, HOPE, AND LOVE

Faith, or belief, is that virtue that resides inside you. This "belief" of yours is as much a part of you as is your soul, mind, and body.

Your belief or faith is a big factor in the make-up of your personality. This is especially the case in the spiritual and mental sectors of your being. **Without faith or belief, nothing exciting will happen in your life. The reason is because you simply do not have the conviction of your goals and plans.**

Strong faith, or belief, generates action and puts the laws of cause and effect in motion, as well as allows unexplainable miracles to occur in your life. **The most important element of faith or belief is this: There is a personal God who will provide guidance and inspiration for you**.

Hope is faith in action. Hope helps us keep our eyes on the goal or end result.

Love is certainly the greatest of virtues.

The best description of love is:

> **"Love is patient, love is kind; love envies not, boasts not, is not haughty, is not rude, is not self-seeking, is not easily provoked, thinks no evil, rejoices not in wrong-doing but rejoices in the truth. Love bears all things, believes all things, hopes all things, endures all things. Love never ends."**

1 Corinthians 13: 4-8 [9]

The power of love truly is limitless.

---

[9] Scripture taken from the NEW AMERICAN STANDARD BIBLE®, Copyright © 1960,1962,1963,1968,1971,1972,1973,1975,1977,1995 by The Lockman Foundation. Used by permission.

CHAPTER 29
BENJAMIN FRANKLIN

It has been written that Benjamin Franklin was not an overly religious man. Who really knows? Yet, look at the virtues he cherished:

1. Temperance
2. Silence
3. Order
4. Resolution
5. Frugality
6. Industry
7. Sincerity
8. Justice
9. Moderation
10. Cleanliness
11. Tranquility
12. Chastity

Also, Benjamin Franklin reviewed his conduct with respect to these virtues on a regular basis.

CHAPTER 30
RE-INVENT YOURSELF

Do you feel a need for a makeover?

Well, you might be right. Determine how extensive your makeover should be.

- Do you wish to change jobs, or career?
- Do you wish to become more spiritual?
- Do you want to improve your physical health and appearance?

Make a list of want you want to accomplish. This is your **things to accomplish list**. It could read like this:

- Get a college degree.
- Start a small business.
- Climb a mountain.
- Start a book review club.
- Get in physical shape.
- Join a church.
- Be/make a friend.
- Be a better person.
- Outline a budget.
- Write a will.

Now, after your list is formulated:

1. **Generate a mission statement**. This explains your "new self."
2. Develop the discipline and tenacity to change.
3. Put a **plan of action** together and write it in your personal journal.
4. **Implement your plan**. That is, actualize and do your plan of action.
5. Get a coach, mentor, or a close friend to help if this is necessary.

CHAPTER 31
CHANGE

Learn to adapt to change, it is the only constant of which you can be sure.

"It is never too late to be who you might have been."
- George Eliot[10], English novelist

"Any change, even a change for the better is always accompanied by drawbacks and discomforts."
- Arnold Bennett[11], English novelist

"If you wait until the wind and weather are just right, you will never plant anything and never harvest anything." - Paraphrased - Ecclesiastes 11:4 [12]

---

[10] Moncur, Michael. The Quotations Page.
http://www.quotationspage.com/quote/31649.html Web. 7 April 2012.

[11] Goodreads, Ind. http://www.goodreads.com/quotes/show/45107 2012. Web. 7 April 2012.

[12] Scripture paraphrased from the NEW AMERICAN STANDARD BIBLE®, Copyright © 1960,1962,1963,1968,1971,1972,1973,1975,1977,1995 by The Lockman Foundation. Used by permission.

CHAPTER 32
RENEWAL/RETREAT

Periodically, it is crucial you review where you are and where you are heading.

This can be both fun and frustrating. No matter, bite the bullet and take the time to do it. The results of this renewal or retreat can be exhilarating and life changing. **A renewal/ retreat program is always worthwhile** as you encounter and deal with reality more intensely, and sometimes more correctly.

To complete a renewal/retreat, review your life (past, present, and future plans), and ask yourself:
- What have you done well?
- What didn't you do so well?
- What didn't you do that you should have done?
- Did you cause ill-feelings with someone?

Use these reflective thoughts to improve the way you are living.

Are you living by the Golden Rule? What should you be doing that will help you now and in the future?

One thing is for sure – do not mull over the mistakes you have made in the past. Mulling over and regretting your mistakes drains energy, enforces negative thinking, wastes time, and brings unwarranted sadness. Part of being a human being on planet earth is making bad choices and mistakes at certain times. Certainly, be sorry for your mistakes and learn from them.

Resolve to move on and actualize your God-given potential. You have done some truly wonderful things in your life. Now, get started and do more things, greater things.

What special mission or assignment do you want to accomplish?
- What are the things you need to do?
- What bad habits must you stop?
- What good habits must you start?

Remember, you get rid of bad habits by replacing them with good habits.

Planning in the present for the future will provide you with a happy, organized, and peaceful life. Seek out someone who can offer specific help or guidance (i.e. mentor or coach).

CHAPTER 33
BE...

Appreciative
Balanced
Charitable
Cheerful
Compassionate
Consistent
Disciplined
Encouraging
Forgiving
Goal-seeking
Hard-working
Helpful
Motivated
Responsible
Supportive
Spiritual

CHAPTER 34
REASONS FOR HAPPINESS

1. Your faith that God loves you and will provide.
2. Realization of all your blessings.
3. Your family and friends and their love.
4. The people willing to help you. Also, the people you can help.
5. The good and wonderful difference you make in the world.
6. You do what you must do – in a timely manner.
7. Knowing you try your best in all situations.
8. You have the ability to do what you want to do.

CHAPTER 35
THOUGHT PROVOKING QUOTES

"You must do the thing you think you cannot do."
-Eleanor Roosevelt[13], American United Nations
Diplomat, Humanitarian, and First Lady, wife of
President Franklin D. Roosevelt

"…our life is what our thoughts make it."
-Marcus Aurelius (121-180 A.D.)[14]

"Life is ten percent what happens to you and ninety percent
how you respond to it."
-Lou Holtz[15], football coach

---

[13] Thinkexist.com.
http://thinkexist.com/quotation/you_must_do_the_thing_you_think_you_cannot/192
388.html Web. 7 April 2012.

[14] Wikiquote. "Marcus Aurelius." http://en.wikiquote.org/wiki/Marcus_Aurelius Web. 7
April 2012.

[15] Quotations Book. http://quotationsbook.com/quote/3468/ Web. 7 April 2012.

"The difference between a successful person and others is not a lack of strength, not a lack of knowledge, but rather a lack of will."
-Vince Lombardi [16]

16 Moncur, Michael. The Quotations Page.
http://www.quotationspage.com/quote/4705.html Web. 7 April 2012.

CHAPTER 36
DOING THESE THINGS MAKES YOU HAPPY

1. Believing in a higher power.
2. Believe and have faith to do great things.
3. Obey basic life tenets.
4. Serve – so you may be served.
5. Love and respect others.
6. Prepare for all your major tasks.
7. Pray.
8. Maintain discipline. Be true to yourself.
9. Budget your time and money.
10. Do what you must do – at the right time.
11. Eat moderately.
12. Council.
13. Be joyous.
14. Be helpful.
15. Appreciate all you have.

CHAPTER 37
STAY MOTIVATED

Stay motivated for the benefit and betterment of:

1. You
2. Your family/loved ones
3. People depending on you and the example you set
4. Your safety and security
5. Your faith
6. Actualizing your potential
7. Doing the right thing
8. Recognition (job or project)
9. Financial considerations

CHAPTER 38
LIFE'S MOUNTAIN

In your life's journey, you sometimes encounter a mountain.

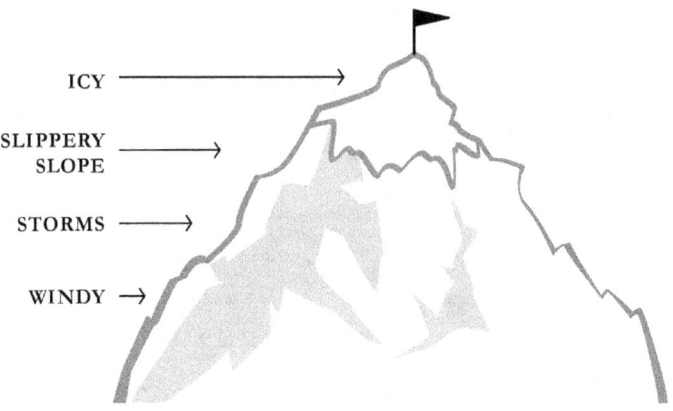

With proper preparation and undaunted effort, you conquer and overcome your mountain.

CHAPTER 39
THINGS TO DO LIST

Copy this form to use as part of your daily routine.
Remember, **stay on course, do your mission**.

1. _____

2. _____

3. _____

4. _____

5. _____

6. _____

7. _____

8. _____

9. _____

10. _____

A brief note on time management:
Time is a very valuable asset. To utilize time most efficiently,
you must: plan your day, prioritize projects, stay focused, and
reward yourself when a particular task is done.

CHAPTER 40
GOAL LIST

Things you want to accomplish in the next 12 months:
(Copy this form to reuse as needed)

1._____

2._____

3._____

4._____

5._____

6._____

7._____

8._____

9._____

Remember to put a time frame on goal achievement.

CHAPTER 41
PERSONAL CHECK CHART

You can make your own check chart to monitor your daily activity. Industry uses such check charts to ensure equipment and processes are operating properly.

Such topics that can be included in your daily check chart are (Copy the following form to reuse as needed):

Week of: ....

	M	T	W	Th	F	Sa	Su
PRAYER							
FAMILY							
DIET							
WORK							
SCHOOL							
CHURCH							
EXERCISE							
READING							
BUSINESS							
PROJECT							

SUMMARY

You are in control of your attitude, virtues, and emotions.

How you manage these elements in your life determines how fulfilling your life will be.

Controlling your attitude, virtues, and emotions is an on-going effort that reaps rewards of achievement, happiness, and well-being.

Remember, "Stay on course, do your mission."

SEMINARS

Tim Penner is available for on-site talks and mini-seminars. Humor is used in the program to make the learning experience more enjoyable.

- Attitude and Virtues
- Retreat/Renewal (Personal or Business)
- Sales/Ethics

Tim Penner
www.timpennerseminars.com
info@timpennerseminars.com

www.ingramcontent.com/pod-product-compliance
Lightning Source LLC
Chambersburg PA
CBHW060003300526
45794CB00003B/1068